# The Badge and the Bible

A UNIQUE DEVOTIONAL

## Kevin J. Fink

NEW HARBOR PRESS

*RAPID CITY, SD*

Fink/New Harbor Press
1601 Mt. Rushmore Rd, Ste 3288
Rapid City, SD 57701
www.NewHarborPress

Ordering Information:
Quantity sales. Special discounts are available on quantity purchases by corporations, associations, and others. For details, contact the "Special Sales Department" at the address above.

The Badge and the Bible / Kevin Fink. -- 1st ed.
ISBN 978-1-63357-430-4

# Contents

# PREFACE

*T*HIS UNIQUE DEVOTIONAL USES personal police stories that bridge to biblical truth and application to hopefully take you deep in the heart of God and encourage you in some way, especially the way of knowing and following the Lord Jesus Christ. Laugh at some of the stories. Be amazed at what law enforcement officers encounter. But, please, use the biblical principles and applications shared. I thank the Lord for giving me the calling, theological education, pastoral experience, and law enforcement background to write this unique devotional.

There are many people to thank on the journey to finally completing the book, especially my wife and children. They encouraged me to write. My wife is a professional woman, a Certified Public Accountant and Finance Director of a large hospital. Our twin boys are grown and gone from home. One is preparing for theological training and ministry, the other is a United States Air

Force Officer. I am deeply grateful to the Lord for giving me an awesome family.

If you are reading this, it means you purchased the book. Thank you. Hopefully, you will be edified in some way. **This unique devotional is meant to be read and used by anyone.**

Scripture quotations are from the New International Version (NIV) of the Bible, and are italicized. THE HOLY BIBLE, NEW INTERNATIONAL VERSION ® , NIV ® , Copyright © 1973, 1978, 1984, 2011 by Biblica, Inc.™ Used by permission. All rights reserved worldwide.

Full biblical references are used. If you are new to navigating Scripture, reference format is as follows - book, followed by chapter, followed by verse. For example: Genesis 1:1 – Genesis is the book, chapter one, verse one.

Not everything on each biblical reference or subject is shared. This book of unique devotions is not an exhaustive theological treatment of subjects addressed. However, sound, consistent hermeneutics, or principles of interpretation, are employed in what is shared from Scripture.

Kevin J. Fink

# INTRODUCTION

*M*OST PEOPLE ARE CAPTIVAT-
ED by the chronicles of law enforcement. Some police encoun-
ters are exciting and dangerous, others sad and
tragic, and still others humorous and amazing.
Police officers encounter all kinds of things and
people. Cops see the best and worst of human
nature and behavior, usually daily. Each duty
shift involves new experiences, at least new in
the sense no two encounters are the same. There
is no such thing as "routine" in the field of law
enforcement. This is in part why police officers
have many stories.

I served in the Nebraska State Patrol several
years before the Lord called me into pastoral
ministry. My primary duty area was Interstate
80 (I-80). Other roads were patrolled, but I-80
was the primary focus due to the amount of traffic. My late father also served in the Nebraska
State Patrol, then was a three-term sheriff of

Nebraska's second largest county, Custer. A late uncle served in the Nebraska State Patrol as well.

Going from the state patrol to ministry was a unique transition, one I believe necessary to share with you in brief before writing further. Only a few days after being informed of selection to the air wing of the state patrol, I was diagnosed with a heart valve condition. This condition had both a blessing and a curse in my life. The curse was that it ended my state patrol career and plunged me into a dark emotional, physical and spiritual abyss for several years. The blessing was that God used the experience to wake me up spiritually and draw me to faith in Jesus. It soon became clear the Lord was leading me into pastoral ministry. Necessary theological education and training were completed, and I served in the Christian and Missionary Alliance as an ordained lead pastor for some two decades before retiring the pulpit. Service to the Lord now involves being the lead chaplain of a large hospital, and I've reengaged the pulpit on a limited basis.

This devotional is not about me, however. Yes, personal stories are shared, but the focus of the book is Jesus and you. Personal encounters merely springboard to biblical principles and application meant to encourage you and take you deep in the heart of the Lord.

A premise in this devotional is the place of authority in society, particularly, in this case, governmental authority in the form of law enforcement. In the New Testament book of Romans, chapter thirteen, verses one-five (Romans 13:1-5), the penman, Paul, wrote about the divine establishment and purpose of civil authority:

> *"Everyone must submit himself to the governing authorities, for there is no authority except that which God has established. The authorities that exist have been established by God. Consequently, he who rebels against the authority is rebelling against what God has instituted, and those who do so will bring judgment on themselves. For rulers hold no terror for those who do right, but for those who do wrong. Do you want to be free from fear of the one in authority? Then do what is right and he will commend you. For he is God's servant to do you good. But if you do wrong, be afraid, for he does not bear the sword for nothing. He is*

*God's servant, an agent of wrath to bring punishment on the wrong-doer. Therefore, it is necessary to submit to the authorities, not only because of possible punishment but also because of conscience."* Peter penned similar words (1 Peter 2:13-17).

Society should have a healthy respect for law enforcement authority and the God who establishes it. Respect and submission should be our mindset toward law enforcement and the God behind law enforcement, even in the presence of bad policing. Paul's words contain no condition, as in, "Submit to authority only if there are no bad cops or bad government influencing the public's trust of cops." In fact, both Paul and Peter penned their commands in the context of a ruthless and godless Roman government, saying, in essence, "You must obey even a bad government, and don't make things worse for yourselves in a godless society by disobeying the government." What of bad police officers? They too should respect the badge they serve; if not, they should be disciplined and/or dismissed.

Only when government asks or demands disobedience to God should it be resisted. *"We must obey God rather than men"* (Acts 5:29).

For example, Christians should disobey a governmental decree of abortion, as abortion violates the principle that life begins at conception (Psalm 139:13-16) and the moral law to not commit murder (Exodus 20:13).

To all law enforcement officers who serve with honor, please read Psalm 91. The jest of the Psalm is that whoever trusts in the Lord finds security and protection, particularly spiritual security and protection. The Psalm is not a promise no harm will ever touch you, but a promise that harm is ineffective against the person who trusts in the Almighty. It's kind of like saying, "You can hit me, kick me, spit on me, call me names, resist me, even kill me, but nothing, absolutely nothing, even death, can separate me from Christ" (Romans 8:38-39).

The greatest security and protection anyone, law enforcement officer to otherwise, can have is Jesus. Take refuge in Him. Trust in Him. Follow Him. Those in Christ are forever safe in His arms. Jesus Himself said, *"I give them eternal life, and they shall never perish; no one can snatch them out of my hand. My Father, who has given them to me, is greater than all; no one can snatch them out of my Father's hand. I and the Father are one"* (John 10:28-30).

Let us be thankful for law enforcement. Law enforcement is needed and appreciated. Though cops are not in a foreign war zone like soldiers, they battle for the safety and well-being of American citizens nonetheless. Their daily battlefield is on American soil. Submit to their authority. Honor their sacrifice. Thank the Lord for establishing police.

Some people think state troopers are merely "Taillight Chasers." That is, all we do is run down speeders. Yes, speed enforcement is a large part of state patrol duties, but speed enforcement is a means to an end. This end is drug confiscation, felony arrests, drunk driver enforcement, and many other things. Stopping someone for speeding is a way to get a closer look at both driver and vehicle, which often yields major things.

Perspective is key to understanding and appreciating different law enforcement roles. For example, a Los Angeles County Sheriff's Deputy assigned to SWAT has a different perspective than a Nebraska State Trooper patrolling I-80 in western Nebraska. I spent part of a day in Los Angeles with the Lieutenant of the sheriff's department emergency services division (SWAT). He asked me, "You patrol miles of interstate by yourself with little or no backup at times?" "Yep," I said. "No way. I wouldn't do it," he remarked. I asked him in turn, "You have an average of two SWAT calls each shift, and have witnessed six officers killed in the line of duty in your career?" "Sadly, yes," he responded. "No way, I wouldn't do it, even if backup were around the corner," I replied. Regarding purpose. His purpose was SWAT. My purpose was traffic enforcement. We were both sworn police officers. No law enforcement officer is better than another, just as no division or jurisdiction or assignment is better than another, only different. All serve the same end – to serve and protect.

The same applies to even old west law enforcement. Lawmen of the west surely had a different perspective than we do today, but their purpose was the same – serve and protect. Personally, it might have been awesome, not to mention dangerous, riding the range as a lawman alongside Bat Masterson, Pat Garrett, Wyatt Earp, or Wild Bill Hickok to stand for right and hunt down bandits and criminals with the only rule of engagement probably being, don't get killed. Let us be grateful for lawmen and lawwomen of all eras, especially our own day.

Only certain law enforcement encounters are shared in this devotional. There is no need to expose you to horrific and gruesome experiences. Neither is every detail of each story shared, only things needed to give you a general picture of what occurred. Also, chapters appear in no special order, save the last one.

# 1

# A HARD TASK

ONE COLD, SNOWY DAY with ice-covered roads, dispatch radioed an injury accident. Upon approaching the accident scene, an overturned utility van was seen. Countless small, white-colored things that appeared to be moving on the roadway were also spotted. Upon a closer look and further investigation, it was discovered the seemingly countless white things were lab mice being transported to a facility in Colorado Springs, Colorado. I hate mice. Mice scampered everywhere, including inside the cab of the van with the trapped driver. Not knowing if the mice were contaminated or not, every fear and emotion had to be put aside to do what needed to be done - swim through the sea of lab mice to reach and extract the driver. It was a hard task.

The mice also made a sickening "popping" sound as other emergency vehicles drove over them while arriving on scene. The task was hard for everyone involved.

*"The Lord sent Nathan to David. When he came to him, he said, 'There were two men in a certain town, one rich and the other poor. The rich man had a very large number of sheep and cattle, but the poor man had nothing except one little ewe lamb he had bought. He raised it, and it grew up with him and his children. It shared his food, drank from his cup and even slept in his arms. It was like a daughter to him. 'Now a traveler came to the rich man, but the rich man refrained from taking one of his own sheep or cattle to prepare a meal for the traveler who had come to him. Instead, he took the ewe lamb that belonged to the poor man and prepared it for the one who had come to him.' David burned with anger against the man and said to Nathan, 'As surely as the Lord lives, the man who did this deserves to die! He must pay for that lamb four times over, because he did such a thing and had no pity.' Then Nathan said to David, you are the man!'"* (2 Samuel 12:1-7). Nathan was as an advisor to King

David, and, though an advisor, a bold confrontation toward a king in that day meant risking one's life. Imagine how hard it was for Nathan do this. He did a hard thing, a risky thing.

What hard task might you be facing today? A hard conversation with a child or coworker or friend or spouse or neighbor? Financial stewardship and living within your budget? Quitting a bad habit? Attending a family reunion that always seems to be messy and difficult? Forgiving someone? Asking someone to forgive you? A sacrifice or change to be a better spouse or parent? Sharing Jesus with a neighbor? Standing in front of a mirror to take an honest look at yourself?

Almost anything can be a hard task.

Hard tasks come with benefits. Doing hard things benefit us by making us stronger, for example. Just as muscle strain makes the body stronger, difficult things strengthen our faith and life (James 1:2-3). So, in a sense, think of hard tasks as weights that make you stronger each time they are lifted. Of course, I don't care to repeat the hard task of swimming amongst mice. I elect to remain weak toward mice!

Maybe the hard thing you're presently wrestling with is coming to faith in Jesus. Jesus understands this, and patiently waits for you to approach Him in faith. It is then you'll find that coming to faith in Jesus is like pressing the easy button on the once popular "The Button" to hear, "That was easy."

# 2

# DUMB, DUMBER AND

# DUMBEST

*T*HIS STORY IS NOT meant to ridicule the people involved. The driver and passenger of a stalled van called the state patrol for help knowing, at least hoping, a uniformed officer would respond. What happened upon arriving was almost unbelievable, at least bewildering. The driver and passenger were smoking marijuana, drug paraphernalia littered the van, and a marijuana joint was still smoldering in the ashtray. After pausing and collecting my thoughts for a moment, I said, "Let me get this right, you broke down, called the state patrol for help (dumbest), and thought the officer would simply ignore the wacky weed and other drug stuff in the van?" (dumber). Then the driver did the dumbest thing still. He responded, "Well, man, we're not driving, and you have a duty to help us." They were about to be helped, only not in the way they hoped. "The good news is that your van is no longer a concern – the state patrol will tow it. The bad news is that both of you are under arrest." The odor of burnt marijuana was so strong in the vehicle and on their persons that a uniform change was necessary after the incident.

> "When tempted, no one should say, 'God is tempting me.' For God cannot be tempted by evil, nor does he tempt anyone; but each one is tempted when, by his own evil desire, he is dragged away and enticed. Then, after desire has conceived, it gives birth to sin; and sin, when it is full-grown, gives birth to death" (James 1:13-15).

Entertaining evil desires is dumb. Acting on such desires is dumber. Allowing evil desires to grow and grow is dumbest still. King David, for example, went from looking with lust upon Bathsheba (dumb) to summoning her (dumber) to hiding his adultery by having her husband killed in battle (dumbest) (2 Samuel 11). All sin is dumb, and it can quickly become dumber and dumbest. One caveat. Though all sin is dumb, not all dumb things are necessarily sinful. For example, grabbing a hot pan on the stove without an oven mitt is dumb, but not sinful. Consider the following examples of sin's progressive nature from dumb to dumber to dumbest.

Sinful anger can turn to hurtful words to hateful actions. Little lies can turn to big lies to multiple lies. Jealousy can turn to silence to distance between you and someone. Pride can turn to more pride to worse pride still. Unforgiveness can turn to a cold heart to a hard heart. Left unchecked, sin always progresses from dumb to dumber to dumbest. Do not allow sin to grow and grow. Rather, confess your sin to the Lord. Do a 180 from sin. Replace sin with goodness, rightness and holiness.

What if you fail? Welcome to the club! Be quick to repent and walk anew on a path that leads you away from whatever it is that is tempting you. For example, if surfing the internet causes you to be tempted by illicit images, install safeguards. Or if the person in the cubicle next to you at work tempts you, quit looking around the corner at every opportunity. Or if you have a heavy foot, as in driving fast, well, set the cruise control at the speed limit. Or if you're in a bad relationship and doing things you ought not be doing, end it before things go further and get worse. Or if bashing the President is a temptation, hold your tongue at the local coffee-shop presidential bash session. Whatever the case, do what is necessary to not fall into the dumb, dumber and dumbest nature of sin. But when you do fall, remember Jesus is there to forgive and cleanse if you confess.

# EVIL HEARTS AND

# INTENTIONS

*I*T HAPPENED ON A moonless night in a rest area. An extremely distressed family in an SUV called the state patrol for immediate help. The father said, "We've been stalked since Arizona; we think it's a cult." Other family members were interviewed separately to determine if the story was valid. Their individual descriptions of the event were similar but not identical (identical testimonies usually indicate something rehearsed). Further investigation identified and located the family's stalkers, who admitted they were trying to exhaust the family to make it easier to force them into their cult. The stalkers had evil hearts and intentions. Thankfully, a terrified family was delivered from the determined clutches of a real and dangerous cult. Other bizarre things related to the incident happened on that dark night as well.

Evil is real. We know evil is present in the world. We look around us and see evil manifest itself in different forms and ways. Do we look at ourselves? We might be quick to judge the stalkers in the above account, and absolutely their actions were wrong and evil, but what of our hearts? God says, *"The heart is deceitful [evil] above all things and beyond cure. Who can understand it?"* (Jeremiah 17:9). This was penned in the context of Jewish leaders who led their people into evil things because their hearts were turned away from God. The deceitful, or evil, hearts of these leaders led themselves and others to ruin. The point is that a heart turned away from God is capable of evil. Any heart is capable of evil, especially a godless heart.

How is your heart? Is your heart for God or against Him? Is your heart turned toward God or away from Him? God knows. He is the only One who understands the heart. Jesus is the only cure for the heart (John 3:3). God wants to give you a new heart (Ezekiel 36:26; Hebrews 8:10) with new desires (Philippians 4:8-9). When a person comes to faith in Jesus, he/she receives a new heart with new desires. New doesn't mean finished or complete, only that God, who knows the heart, then begins to work to make the heart more and more godly. In other words, in Christ

we're made new then grow to realize this new-
ness more and more.

This does not mean a believer in Christ never
does evil things, only a believer is quick to repent and hopefully grow in Christ to sin less and
less. Just as we put away childish things as we
grow into adulthood, so we should progressively
put away sin as we grow in Jesus. In other words,
Christians are not sinless, but we should sin less.
The evil desires and intentions of our hearts
should be continually and increasingly replaced
with good and godly desires and intentions.
When evil desires pop up in your heart, think
of godly things instead. For example, instead of
road rage, consider patience and understanding. To be personal and open, I admit aggrava-
tion with bad drivers. They enrage me at times.
Thankfully, I'm doing better at being patient and
understanding.

# RECEIVE GOOD COUNSEL

*U*PON TAKING A NEEDED break from investigating accidents during a night snowstorm, a family approached at a restaurant to ask, "Can we make it west? We need to get to Colorado for a snow skiing vacation." I graciously responded, "Multiple vehicles are in the ditch waiting to be towed. Travel is hazardous. Many accidents have already occurred. Travel is not advised. Be safe. Get a motel room for the night." The father said, "Okay, thanks for the report" as the family left the restaurant. Dispatch later called reporting, "Family stranded in snow due to accident." Yep, it was the family from the restaurant. Thankfully, no one was injured, but they did have to be transported to a motel, where they stayed for two days before their vehicle could be removed from the snowy median. The family's ski trip took place in a boring motel room instead of breathtaking mountain slopes in Colorado. It's imagined that one or more of the family members said to the father in the motel room, "Yep, we should have listened to the trooper's counsel."

The Bible has a lot to say about receiving good counsel. For example, the Book of Proverbs is saturated with the subject. Here is one of many texts in the book that highlight the importance of receiving good counsel: *The way of a fool seems right to him, but a wise man listens to advice*" (Proverbs 12:15).

How many of us were fools as young people, not receiving the good counsel of our parents? If only we had been wise and listened to dad and mom, wow, could we have been spared some hard knocks. We know what the "way of a fool" means. Consider God is the ultimate parent. How many of us still behave foolishly, not receiving the good counsel of His word as recorded in Scripture? For example, God tells us to "*tame the tongue*" (James 1:26). Do we receive this counsel or do we act foolishly and lash out at someone? Surely, like the family in the above account, after something bad happens because we didn't listen, we think, "Yep, I should have listened to God's word."

Seminary counseling class was difficult. It involved complex steps to giving advice to others. Thus, after passing the class, I narrowed these difficult and complex steps to three work-able ones: 1) Surrender yourself to Jesus; 2) Submerse yourself in God's word; 3) Surround yourself with God's people. In other words, trust in Christ fully, live God's word completely, and be involved in the fellowship and life of a Jesus-centered church always. This is not meant to oversimplify counseling, only bring it to a level that's understandable and doable for most people. Nor do these three steps ignore psychol-ogy. Theology is truth, whereas psychology aids in the application of truth. For example, good theological counsel says to think with the mind of Christ (Philippians 2) and psychology aids this by helping us better understand the mind and behaviors.

Good counsel should be received. How do we know if counsel is good? Good counsel is based on truth, be it the truth found in God's word or truth found in psychology or somewhere else. All truth is God's truth. In addition, God has giv-en us an internal barometer of right and wrong. We intuitively know what's good and bad. Pay attention to this barometer, especially if oth-ers are confirming it through good counsel. For example, we know in our hearts that stealing is wrong, so pay attention when a fellow student might say, "Hey, plagiarism is stealing" or a cop

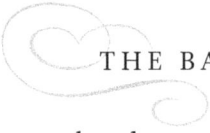

on break says, "Don't drive on the hazardous roads that you already know are impassible."

5

# OWN YOUR SIN

NE EARLY SUMMER MORNING as the sun peeked over the eastern horizon, radar clocked a car at 90 MPH. "Really? The driver must be trying to outrun the sunrise," I thought. A chase ensued when the driver of the car realized the state patrol was coming upon him hard and fast. Finally realizing he could not outrun the state patrol, the driver stopped, and three people jumped from the vehicle (two girls and one boy). All three occupants of the car were runaways from another state. These youngsters were trying to escape consequences of their bad behavior back home. The two girls were armed. One girl had a knife, the other a loaded revolver. The young man was not armed, but physically resisted arrest. The young man and two girls should have owned their sin back home. They would have faced consequences in their respective areas of residence, but nothing like they were about to face for fleeing to avoid arrest, resisting arrest, reckless driving, and carrying illegal, concealed weapons. These three youngsters blame shifted as well, each saying, "The others made me do it."

*"The man said, 'The woman you put here with me — she gave me some fruit from the tree, and I ate it.' Then the Lord God said to the woman, 'What is this you have done?' The woman said, 'The serpent deceived me, and I ate'"* (Genesis 3:12-13). The context reveals that God told Adam and Eve not to eat from the fruit of this tree, but they disobeyed, then shifted blame. Adam blamed Eve, Eve in turn blamed the serpent. Neither Adam nor Eve owned their sin, at least not at first.

We should respond to personal sin this way: "Yep, it was me. I did it!" Instead, often we respond as Adam and Eve did to God: "It was the other person, not me." We may not actually say this, but its reality in thought is nonetheless real. A good test regarding owning our own sin is this: "Do I find it easier to identify my own sin or someone else's sin?" If the latter, I may be trying to blame shift or hide my sin. It could be that I am also falling into the trap of comparing myself to others, "Well, I'm not as bad as that person." That's yet another way of casting blame elsewhere. God expects us to own our own sin. This does not mean we never evaluate the lives of others, like identifying problem areas in our children's lives to better raise them, only that evaluation must begin with us.

First and foremost, we must, as Scripture says, *"Take the log out of my own eye. . ."* (Matthew 7:5). Some of us have a big log in our eyes at times. God has a lot of work to do on our own hearts without us worrying about the hearts of others. The Lord wants us to own our own sin before we attempt to get other people to own their sin. The sin meter should point at us before it moves to others.

My oldest twin son by ten minutes once got a small twig stuck in his right eyeball while playing with friends in a tree. It was a traumatic experience for all of us, especially him. He understandably screamed and cried through it all. Oh, and I far exceeded the speed limit rushing him to the emergency room twenty miles away. Thankfully, thc twig was rcmovcd, and his eye suffered no permanent damage. What if we treated sin like my son's twig in his eye? That is, we screamed and cried for God to take it out. This is the idea behind taking the log out of our own eyes. Ask God to urgently take sin out of your eyes. Cry out to the Lord for the removal of sin from your soul. Shout to the Father above that you're owning your own sin.

# 6

# YES, THE LAW SAYS THIS

*V*IOLATORS SOMETIMES SAY, "I don't think the law says that." They did not want the law to say that. The "that" in one instance was enforcing the Nebraska law that prohibits pedestrians on the Interstate. Some states allow this, but Nebraska does not. It is illegal in Nebraska to hitchhike from the Interstate. Upon sharing this law with a particular hitchhiker on the Interstate, he responded, "The law doesn't say that. I can hitchhike wherever I want. After all, it's America – the Land of the Free." He heard in response, "The law does say you can hitchhike, just not from the Interstate. American freedom does not mean you are free to break the law." Then things got weird and wild. Upon being asked what he did for a job, the hitchhiker responded with a wild look and profane language, "I'm an executioner, and your next!" At this point his hitchhiking on the Interstate was not a concern. This hitchhiker was about to learn that the law also says several other things, like you cannot maliciously threaten a police officer. The law was being brought to bear on a bad person and bad situation. The law was penetrating a man's evil heart and intentions.

> *"For the word of God is living and active. Sharper than any double-edged sword, it penetrates even to dividing soul and spirit, joints and marrow; it judges the thoughts and attitudes of the heart. Nothing in all creation is hidden from God's sight. Everything is uncovered and laid bare before the eyes of him to whom we must give account"* (Hebrews 4:12-13).

God's word says what it says. We may not like what Scripture says in places, like when it pricks our hearts, but this is part of its "living and active" nature. The truth of the Bible penetrates our lives in an active way, working in us and changing us. It reveals what lies deep inside the heart, which God sees clearly. In other words, like a parent sees the heart of his/her children, who are accountable to rules of the home, God sees our hearts, and we're accountable to His word, even the places we may respond, "I do not think it says that" or "I do not want it to say that."

Dive into the Bible and let it change you. Read Scripture. Study Scripture. Live the word of God. Invite God to penetrate your inner thoughts and motives through His word. God knows your thoughts and motives anyway, so allow Him to reveal them to you through what He says in Scripture. And do not be surprised when the pointed, or sharp, truth of the Bible cuts at your heart, saying, if you will, "Yes, it really says this." For example, God's word really says, *"Husbands, love your wives, just as Christ loved the church and gave himself up for her"* (Ephesians 5:25). Oh boy, that penetrates! Scripture in turn tells wives to "respect their husbands" (Ephesians 5:33). That penetrates too. Scripture always penetrates.

As lead chaplain of a large hospital, I see many trauma patients saved by the skilled hands of doctors and nurses. These medical professionals use tools and techniques to penetrate a person's body to hopefully save their lives. For example, an emergency CT scan provides detailed, internal information. If you will, Scripture is the CT scan of the soul. God uses it to see deep in the soul and hopefully bring us to saving faith in Christ and increased growth in Christ. It's all for our good, just as emergency medical procedures are for the good of the patient. Invite Jesus and His word to penetrate your heart and life.

# 7

# PAYBACK DOES NOT PAY

THERE WERE SEVERAL TIMES re-paying evil for evil or insult for in-sult was considered. For example, while slowing traffic a few hundred yards back from where another trooper was investigating an injury accident, a driver sped by as he yelled obscenities out the window at me. The driver also used sign language! I wanted to run the driver down to repay him in some way. On an-other occasion a male suspect physically abused a female victim. I wanted to say to him, "So you think you're a tough guy? Why don't you try that on me?" Then there's the time a fellow trooper got covered in cow manure and urine as he walked too close to the trailer of a truck hauling cattle. He was covered from hat to shoes in animal yuck. I happened to be there, and, oh, did I laugh. The fellow trooper was not so cheer-ful, however. He wanted some type of payback against the truck driver, which he never got be-cause he had to rush home to change uniforms.

In these cases, payback would have made things worse. Payback does not pay.

*"Do not repay evil with evil or insult with insult, but with blessing, because to this you were called so that you may inherit a blessing"* (1 Peter 3:9). Paul penned similar words in Romans 12:17-19. Peter is simply telling Christians how they should respond to others who may do bad or evil things to them. Do not retaliate. Do not seek revenge. Do not be hostile toward those who are hostile toward you. How many of us secretly plot against someone for harming us? We want payback. When something bad happens to the person, whether by our hand or someone else's hand or they experience a bad situation or trial, we may inwardly think, "They got what they deserve. This serves them right." Such a mindset is not Christlike. Instead, we should love the person, pray for the person, do good things for the person, and attempt to live at peace with him/ her.

Is there someone you want to get even with, someone you want to settle the score with? Give it to Christ. Let Jesus have vengeance if there is to be any. The beauty of giving revenge or payback to the Lord is that the desire for them fades as we focus on Christ. Look to Jesus, not at the person or situation. If you are to burn with something, burn with desire for Christ and living a Christlike life.

This is not to say people who wrong us or do bad things to us should not be held accountable, only that we should not seek retaliation, revenge or payback. The person who seeks to catch another person in a mousetrap often ends up in the trap himself. What he hoped would harm the other person ends up harming himself instead. This is also the trap of anger. Unresolved anger, like seeking payback, serves to harm the person who harbors it. Unsettled anger is an internal flame that burns the soul. Can anger be controlled? Yes. There is a healthy way to handle anger. The way to control anger is to not let it control you (Ephesians 4:26-27). Give anger to Jesus. Ask Christ to help you turn from anger to forgiveness. Forgiving others will release you from the mousetrap of revenge and the harmful flame of anger. You might ask, "How do I forgive?" Forgiveness is an act of the will. You must choose to forgive.

# 8

# BE COURAGEOUS

THE FOLLOWING ACCOUNT TOOK place on a moonless night at a ranch far from anywhere. The report said that a ranch employee was threatening to shoot his family then himself with a high-powered rifle. The man also told dispatch that he would shoot any vehicle coming down his driveway. I called for backup as I sped to the start of the family's two-mile driveway. An action plan was discussed when the other trooper arrived. We would speed in and overwhelm the man with force. Of course, speeding in with headlights on meant making ourselves visible targets, especially the patrol car in the lead. Knowing this danger, the other trooper responded with a little chuckle in this voice, "The report went to you, so you go first!" I was scared, but courageous, and went first. It was my duty. Thankfully, the incident ended with no one being harmed, but, wow, was I on-edge driving down that long driveway expecting a bullet from a rifle at any moment. Police officers are often put in harm's way, even run into harm if necessary. When most people run from danger, law enforcement officers run into danger. This requires great courage.

> *"Be strong and courageous, because you will lead these people to inherit the land I swore to their forefathers to give them. Be strong and very courageous. Be careful to obey all the law my servant Moses gave you; do not turn from it to the right or to the left, that you may be successful wherever you go. Do not let this Book of the Law depart from your mouth; meditate on it day and night, so that you may be careful to do everything written in it. Then you will be prosperous and successful. Have I not commanded you? Be strong and courageous. Do not be terrified; do not be discouraged, for the Lord your God will be with you wherever you go"* (Joshua 1:6-9).

Moses died, and now Joshua was assuming leadership of Israel. Inheriting the land (i.e., Canaan) involved war. Joshua would have to conquer the land. He thus needed great strength and courage, along with a reminder that God was always with him.

What courageous thing might God be asking you to do? Courage is not the absence of fear, but the ability to move forward in fear. Courage is required for a lot of things Christians are commanded and expected to do, like sharing Jesus with someone, forgiving someone, speaking truth when we know it will result in personal attack or persecution, loving a cantankerous neighbor, fleeing temptation, holding one another accountable, reconciliation with someone, holding fast to the truth of God's word in a relativistic society, not gossiping at the coffee shop, speaking with grace, restoring backsliders. confessing our sin, and many other things. These things can have an element of fear, but courage moves forward in fear to do what needs to be done. Cops do this multiple times each day. They courageously move forward in fear on each call, each stop, each case, each situation, some more harrowing than others.

Faith itself may require the most courage. Taking the first step toward something can demand great bravery. Then momentum helps move us forward, but, oh, the first step can be difficult. Courage starts with the first step. Take the first step of faith toward whatever it is God is asking you to do. Momentum in Christ will help you the rest of the way. Maybe your first step needs to be faith in Jesus. I encourage you to take it. Remember your first step into a swimming pool in swimming lessons? It may have been quite frightful for you. Then you discovered it wasn't so bad, and soon you were learning to dive off the high board into the deep end of the pool. Take the first step toward Jesus, and soon you'll be navigating the deeper things of Christ and His word.

# STRANGE VOICES

A NAKED MAN WAS WALKING along the Interstate in daylight hours for all passing motorists to see. Upon approaching the man and inquiring why he was naked, he said, "I hear voices telling me that aliens are coming, and they want me nude for arrival in my new home with them." The troubled man went on to talk about his new friends who, he said, often spoke to him. He even commented at one point, "They are talking right now. Hear them?" The man was transported to a facility where he could receive professional help and, wow, was he mad. He shouted, "You're ruining my alien abduction experience. I'm ready. I want to be with them." The man did hear voices - strange voices.

The following principle comes not from a certain passage of Scripture but a study of the whole. There are only three voices in the world: God; Satan; and/or man. God's voice is clearly revealed in Scripture. Thus, if a voice does not align with the truth of God's word or truth itself, the voice is not coming from Him but from either Satan and/or man. For example, God clearly tells us there is only one way to heaven – Jesus. Satan tells us lies to try to blind us to this truth. And man, well, man muddies the water further by thinking heaven has multiple paths – whatever seems right to the individual. Unlike a geographical location on earth that can be reached by many ways, heaven is reached by only one road – faith in Christ. Satan and/or man also try to get us to believe that God's voice is the strange voice, as if to say, "Don't listen to what God says."

God's voice is not strange. His voice may be strange to unbelievers, but not to those who follow Christ: *"My sheep hear my voice, and I know them, they follow me"* (John 10:27). Evaluate all voices by the clear and divine voice of Scripture. Test everything by the word of God. Like a child clearly knows and follows the voice of his/her parents, believers in Jesus know and follow God's voice in Scripture, at least can and should anyway. Pick up the Bible and listen to God's voice. It will help you identify and navigate strange voices.

Just as law enforcement officers learn to pay attention to gut-feelings, Christians must learn to heed warning indicators the Spirit provides through the word of God. For example, if a voice on television or radio or in a book or through the internet, whatever the place, is telling you that you are not beautiful, do not listen, for God says that you are *"fearfully and wonderfully made"* (Psalm 139:14). Or ignore the voice that may say, "There is no harm in a little sinful pleasure," for God says, *"Do not be deceived: God cannot be mocked. A man reaps what he sows"* (Galatians 6:7). Or maybe someone says, "Trash-talk your parents," but God says, *"Honor your father and mother"* (Exodus 20:12). Or, "If you had a bad past you can have only a bad future," but God says, *"Anyone in Christ is a new creation; the old is gone, the new has come"* (2 Corinthians 5:17).

Sometimes we need to unplug to hear God's voice in Scripture. We need time to disengage our noisy world to better hear the voice of God. The Psalmist said, *"Be still and know that I am God"* (Psalm 46:10). You will hear God's voice better as you make time to sit and listen without distractions. Periodically set aside whatever creates noise in your life to contemplate the Lord and His word. Doing this is also good for the body and mind. Spending time with Jesus in His word will keep you from walking down the roadway naked with aliens about you!

# 10

# PRIDE AND PUNISHMENT

THE FEMALE DRIVER OF a car stopped for speeding handed an "Attorney at Law" card out her window as if to pridefully say, "You best not give me a ticket." Her game was recognized and played. She was given a warning. She smiled pridefully, as if to say, "I knew that would work." Well, I knew her well. I knew she would again speed when out of sight. So, a VASCAR clock was started as soon as her wheels began to move. VASCAR is an acronym for Visual Average Speed Computer and Recorder, a tool that measures time and distance very accurately. Sitting long enough for her to get out of sight, I raced to find her in traffic again and complete the clock. Her speed increased 10 MPH over the initial clock. "Mam, you were clocked this time with VASCAR, and will receive a speeding citation." She said nothing, and most definitely did not hand her attorney card out the window again. Her pride brought punishment.

*"Pride goes before destruction, a haughty spirit before a fall"* (Proverbs 16:18). The principle here is that pride leads to downfall. Remember in school when you may have thought, "I'm smart. I do not need to study. I got this test." Then, amazingly, you bombed the exam. That was pride working. Whatever the form of pride, it leads to a fall of some kind. Is there a cure for pride?

The cure for pride is humility. Scripture says, *"Clothe yourselves with humility toward one another, because God opposes the proud and gives grace to the humble"* (1 Peter 5:5). We all know what it means to be clothed. What garment do you wear – pride or humility? Do other people see you dressed in pride or dressed in humility? What does God see? Humility is not seeing oneself as worthless, but dependent on God. Humility does not belittle oneself, but lifts others up. In practice, a humble person focuses on God and others more than self. One caveat. There's a form of pride called false humility, which is basically a person trying to appear humble to impress others. This form of pride usually involves something that communicates to others, "Look how humble I am."

The greatest example of humility is Jesus, and we are called to have His humble attitude

(Philippians 2:5-8). Read this passage, as it says a lot about what true humility looks like. Maybe you need to humble yourself before God and believe in Jesus. It takes humility to acknowledge one's sinfulness before God and trust in His Son, who died for your sins. Humility says to God, "I cannot save myself. I cannot fix my lost, broken soul. I am a sinner in need of the Savior. Only He can save me and fix me." The Scriptures clearly declare and history records that *"Jesus died for our sins, then was buried, then rose from the dead on the third day"* (paraphrase of 1 Corinthians 15:1-3). *"The person who believes in Jesus will not be punished but have eternal life"* (paraphrase of John 3:16). Don't let pride keep you from believing in Jesus. Don't suffer enteral punishment because pride came between you and Christ. Humble yourself before the Lord, believing in Him for the forgiveness of your sins and eternal life.

Most of us know what it's like to be too proud to ask someone for help. Most Americans have experienced this because it's an American mindset – "Not me, I don't need help." We do need help, especially spiritual help from Jesus. Our mindset toward Christ should be, "Yes me, I absolutely need You."

# 11

# LAST BREATH

*I* HAVE BEEN WITH MANY people during their last breath on this earth. Whether by an accident or the end of a long illness, sudden or expected, young or old, they inhaled and exhaled for the final time. One person was my father. I was home on leave from the state patrol when my father suffered a massive, fatal heart attack. I performed CPR with no success, watching and hearing my dad take his last breath. Though a difficult situation, I was thankful to be there with dad and for dad. It was also good to be there with my grieving and shaken mother. The truth that everyone will take a last breath on earth hit me hard that day.

> *"Just as man is destined to die once, and after that to face judgment, so Christ was sacrificed once to take away the sins of many people; and he will appear a second time, not to bear sin, but to bring salvation*

*to those who are waiting for him"*
(Hebrews 9:27-28).

We do not know when or in what circumstances our end with come, only that it will come. Death is an unyielding reality. Thankfully, just as Jesus died only once for our sins, so we experience death only one time. Two things happen at death for a Christian. These things don't happen sequentially or apart, but at the same moment in time: 1) The body falls to the ground like a tent being taken down (2 Corinthians 5:1-9); 2) The soul rises to be with Jesus (Acts 7:54-60).

How should we prepare for our inevitable last breath on this earth? Most people don't like to think about death, but it seems foolish to not consider something that's imminent. Preparing for death includes many things, like having a will, outlining a funeral service, designating power of attorney, having a master file at home or some safe place, and other things, but the all-important preparation for death is making sure you are right with Jesus. I'm not lessening Jesus to a to-do-list but highlighting Him as the most important matter in life and death. Christ is not a death insurance policy or checklist, but the Life-Giver now and forever.

The life Jesus freely offers you begins today and extends beyond the grave to eternity. Jesus said, "*I am the resurrection and the life. He who believes in me will live, even though he dies; and whoever lives and believes in me will never die. Do you believe this?*" (John 11:25-26). Jesus does not promise the absence of physical death, but the assurance of spiritual life beyond the grave. It is kind of like saying, "Our last breath here is our first in heaven!" Therefore, as Paul said, "*To live is Christ and to die is gain*" (Philippians 1:21). You can be assured of this gain today by trusting in Jesus. We cannot keep this life, but we can never lose eternal life in Christ. Prepare for your last breath on earth by taking your first breath in Christ, that is, believe in Him as your Savior.

A similar but different subject is praying for physical healing. Does God heal physically? Of course. Does God always heal physically? No. Along with the theology of healing there is also the theology of dying and death. Where does a prayer of faith come in (James 5:13-18)? Think of CPR. We are called to act by performing CPR if someone drops over, and we believe our actions will have positive results. Likewise, we are called to act by praying for a sick person to be healed, believing our prayers will have positive results. In either case – CPR or prayer, the

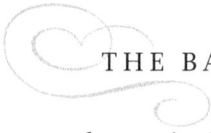

results are in God's hands. We do our part. God does His.

# 12

# TRIAGE

*O*NE OF THE HARDER things to do, at least in my mind and experience, is assign degrees of urgency to car accident victims to decide order of treatment. This is called triage. One story stands out. It involved two young people, male and female. The male victim was trapped in the seatbelt of his overturned car and struggling to breath because of a collapsed lung. He could be saved if removed immediately from his restraint. The female victim was thrown from the car against a large fence post, sustaining a serious head injury. It was doubtful she would survive. I was alone. What should I do? Who should I try to save? Doing nothing was not an option. Better to save one life than lose two lives. The man was saved, the girl died. Pray for people and professions who must make hard triage decisions.

A form of triage can also be used when assigning degrees of urgency to problems. Triage is a good way to navigate and manage the seemingly endless trials we go through in life. Moses, for example, practiced a form of triage when leading the people of Israel. He handled hard matters while other assigned leaders dealt with lesser issues. We might also call this good leadership or delegation of responsibilities. Jethro, Moses' father-in-law, gave him advise on how to triage problems, saying, *"Select capable men from all the people - men who fear God, trustworthy men who hate dishonest gain - and appoint them as officials over thousands, hundreds, fifties and tens. Have them serve as judges for the people at all times, but have them bring every difficult case to you; the simple cases they can decide themselves. That will make your load lighter, because they will share it with you."* (Exodus 18:21-22).

Sometimes we procrastinate in dealing with problems because there seems to be too many. "How will we ever get through," we think. Problems do seem to come in waves. What do we do? Being idle is not the answer. Becoming paralyzed by problems is not the answer. Ignoring them is not the answer. Hoping things will get better is not the answer. The problem with problems is that they usually do not go away on their own but worsen without attention. We must act to bring resolution to problems, at least ones we can control. Use triage to help manage your problems. Like Moses, prioritize problems. For example, what needs immediate attention – putting out the fire on the stove or plunging the stool that is running over? Or if your paycheck is consistently short, do you continue publication subscriptions or buy groceries? Common sense often dictates best triage.

What problems are you up against today? List them if it helps. Now look at the list carefully. Which problems need immediate attention? Handle those first. Then address the next level of problems and so on. If your list grows to the size of a grocery list, well, maybe just go shopping! When overwhelmed in the pastorate with church issues, not knowing where to even start addressing them, I went coyote hunting. Sitting alone outside in nature waiting and hoping a coyote would respond to my call was good for my soul. I often came away from these times with greater clarity of mind and ready to deal with any problem(s). So, yes, if needed, go shopping. Do whatever it is that helps clear or reset your mind. Include yourself in triage.

# 13

# PATIENCE

WE ALL HAVE FAVORITE things – favorite color, favorite flavor, favorite TV show, favorite vacation, etc. I had a favorite VASCAR perch. Like wolves run in packs, speeders often drive in groups. The practice of waiting and watching for the packs took patience, but experience told me they were coming. After clocking all cars in the pack, I would race ahead of them a half-mile or so, jump out of my unit, stand in middle of the road, and point them over to the side one by one. Oh, how I enjoyed hunting the packs. Again, it took patience. Most things do. The highest speed I ever clocked was 145 mph!

*"As God's chosen people, holy and dearly loved, clothe yourselves with compassion, kindness, humility, gentleness and patience"* (Colossians 3:12). We all understand what it means to be clothed. The context of this passage is that Christians are to get rid of the old garments of sin to be clothed with Christlikeness, which includes the things

listed here in the passage, like patience. *Do not let the word "chosen" in the passage confuse you; it simply means those who trust in Christ. Admittedly, patience is a garment that's sometimes hard to wear or it just hangs in the closet collecting dust.

What kind of clothes do you leave your home in each day? Most of us take considerable time bathing, grooming and clothing ourselves in the morning. What of spiritual garments, like patience? Is patience part of your daily attire? Do you take time to put on patience? Do you exhibit patience toward your spouse, your children, your friends, your neighbors, your boss, your coworkers, your friends, etc.? Do you show patience toward those who do not think like you, believe like you, behave like you? Are you allowing others time and room to grow? A wise, older pastor now gone to heaven gave this challenge, "How long did it take God to get your attention?" I responded, "Twenty-nine years." The pastor remarked, "Well, be patient with others and give them at least the same amount of time" (A. J. Knickerbocker).

I do not know how you need to show patience today, only that you do, as we all must. If you are like me, even though I may be clothed in patience, I do not always practice it well.

Impatience sometimes shows its soiled garb over the clean apparel of patience. When impatience surfaces, we need to consider the great patience of Christ toward us (2 Peter 3:15). Just as Jesus is patient with us, we need to be patient with others, maybe even patient with ourselves. Let us learn and practice patience, the patience of Christ, who Scripture says is "long-suffering" (2 Peter 3:9).

Think of a rubber band that can be stretched to extreme lengths without breaking. Ideal patience is a rubber band that can be tested to great lengths without failing. Don't let patience snap. What if patience does break? When we blow being patient, let us put the garment of patience back on afresh and anew resolving in the strength of Christ do better. Reset the rubber band to be stretched again.

Jesus is patiently waiting for you to trust in Him. His patience will not run out, but your time will. Death seals our eternal destination, and because no one knows their hour of passing from this earth, trust in Jesus today. Do not delay. Do not put off making the most important decision and commitment of your life – Jesus.

# BAD COMPANY

*A*CAR WITH SIX MEN turned out to be a matter of bad company for one occupant. This person was attempting to hide an odd-looking object between his legs that stretched from the floorboard to his knees in height. The object was a homemade weapon of sorts. It looked like something out of a science fiction movie. This weird weapon had a curved wooden handle with a sharpened axe head and two double-edged knives, all wrapped in leather and lace with silver studs. This person agreed to hide the weapon as the car pulled over for the stop. As it turned out, he did so because several other passengers were wanted on felony warrants. This otherwise innocent person was influenced by bad company. Such was the case often. We all know this dynamic as guilt by association.

*"Do not be misled: 'Bad company corrupts good character'"* (1 Corinthians 15:33). Paul penned this in the context of Christians hanging with

people who denied the resurrection. They influenced some Christians to question the most fundamental Christian doctrine. In other words, "Hanging with heretics corrupts sound beliefs." This principle extends to many things, not just the dangers of heresy. For example, just as standing too close to a fire will get you burned, so being with bad company will harm you. Or to break a literary rule and switch to another analogy – just as touching wet paint taints one's hands, so bad company taints one's character, attitude and behavior.

Who do you hang with? We should distance ourselves from bad company, whoever and whatever it is. This does not mean we should never associate with bad company, for even Jesus associated at times with bad people (e.g., Mark 2:16-17), only that we must be careful not to allow their bad character to taint us. So, choose your friends wisely. Practically speaking, if you find yourself in a car cruising town with occupants who insist on drinking, get out of the car as soon as possible. Or you are at a party when drugs arrive, leave the party immediately. Or a friend has bad behavior in general, draw some boundaries in the friendship. Or someone is trying to get you to go along with something bad and wrong, make your "no" clear and distance yourself from the person and situation. It may even be that you need different friends or company! Still, at some point bad people need to be befriended by a Christian to hear the changing and saving Gospel of Jesus Christ. Jesus loves even persons of bad character.

Jesus specializes in bad people - sinners, like you and me. But Christ wants to change us. Do Christians evidence bad behavior at times? Yes. The bad company that may be influencing someone could be me! *The difference between Christians and non-Christians is not necessarily the absence of sin but the presence of repentance. Christians can and should recognize sin in their lives, confess and repent, and walk anew in Christ. We should not, if you will, remain in a car filled with hoodlums. We shouldn't let them talk us into doing something stupid either. Whatever the case, don't be tied closely with people of bad character.

# TEMPTATION CAN BE

# STRONG

*A* DEPUTY ASKED TO MEET at a certain motel to see something special in the parking lot. The special something was a Lamborghini, a fast and expensive Italian sports car. Lamborghinis have a large, powerful engine capable of speeds more than 200 MPH. There we were, admiring this beautiful machine. Then an older man walked up, "I see you like my car." "Absolutely," we responded. After some small-talk, the owner of the car showed us the twelve-cylinder engine, and as he held out the keys, asked, "Do you want to take it for a spin?" Wow, did I want to drive it! I pictured myself cruising down I-80 at 200 MPH like a NASCAR driver, only in a state patrol uniform. The temptation was strong. Neither the deputy nor I got behind the wheel of the Lamborghini, but we did ask the man how fast he had drove it. The older gentleman responded with a grin, "Once in Arizona I hit 180 MPH with plenty of pedal to go, but the Arizona State Patrol busted me using aircraft. It cost me almost a thousand dollars." The owner of the car should have resisted to drive his car at speeds some helicopters and small planes fly, just as the deputy and I resisted the temptation to take it for a spin on I-80.

P. S. What would I do if given the opportunity again? Probably take the car for a spin, only I would promise not to break the speed limit (yeah, right!).

> *"No temptation has seized you except what is common to man. And God is faithful; he will not let you be tempted beyond what you can bear. But when you are tempted, he will also provide a way out so that you can stand up under it"* (1 Corinthians 10:13).

Everyone experiences temptation. Temptation is common to all people. No one is exempt from sin's lure. Sinful enticement itself is not sin, though, acting on it is. Thankfully, God does not allow us to be tempted to the point of giving in. He provides an escape route. Therefore, there is no temptation that we cannot resist. The temptation may be strong, but we can stand against it in God's strength and provision.

Run! Take God's provided escape route away from temptation. Just as law enforcement and emergency personnel detour traffic away from an accident, God detours us away from temptation. Pay attention to the Lord's provided detours away from temptation. He is trying to spare you the pain and consequences of giving in. Again, take the God-provided route, path or detour away from whatever may be tempting you. For example, if a beautiful or handsome person tempts you as she/he walks by, divert your gaze. Or if you're tempted to have sex outside marriage with someone, use the path of keeping your clothes on. Or if the temptation of greed seizes you, travel the road of contentment. Or if you are tempted to cover up something with a lie, take the path of telling the truth. Most detours around temptation involve common sense, like switching the channel if a television program contains tempting images or messages.

What happens when we allow temptation to turn to sin? Consequences! Though Jesus does not spare us from the consequences of our sin, thankfully, He does promise to forgive us if we ask. Ask. My late father always said, "Son, ask if you need help." The same is true with Christ. For example, "Lord, I can't resist temptation on my own, please help me." Or "Lord, I've failed again, please forgive me." Like any good father,

God is always ready and willing to respond to our requests.

# 16

# LAUGH

ISPATCH CALLED IN THE early morning hours to assist a county sheriff in the investigation of a non-injury truck accident. Like a fighter pilot scrambling to his jet in an emergency, I hurriedly dressed and left the house with no thought of taking time to do necessary business in the bathroom. After several hours of accident investigation, it became quite clear that a bowel movement was imminent. There was no holding it this time. Where do I go? No trees. No brush. No buildings. Just wide-open cattle country. My car would get stuck in the sandy pastures. But my bowels didn't care. They were about to burst where I stood. "Ah, the sheriff's 4x4 pickup," I thought. I scurried to his pickup, jumped in, and tore out across a pasture over a hill to do what should have been done before leaving the house. Everything was great, except on thing. I could not find the switch that controlled the pickup's emergency lights. Imagine the scene. A state trooper driving a sheriff's pickup furiously through a pasture and over a hill with emergency lights flashing so he could urgently have relief. But there I was – over a hill, gun belt laid on the hood of the pickup, emergency lights flashing, uniform pants dropped to my ankles, doing you know what. Oh, toilet paper is another part of the story, but I'll just leave it at that. As I came back over the hill and reentered the highway by the accident scene, the sheriff, a wrecker crew, other emergency responders, and onlookers all applauded me while laughing. I laughed too. Who wouldn't laugh? Everyone had a good chuckle.

*"A cheerful heart is good medicine, but a crushed spirit dries up the bones"* (Proverbs 17:22). Part of having a cheerful heart is laughter. Appropriate laughter is good for the body, as well as the soul. Laughter is a win, win.

Laugh! Even laugh at yourself. When something has you down or crushed, take the medicine of laughter. Laughter is good medicine anytime, even when we are not suffering. Obviously, there is a time to laugh and a time to not laugh (Ecclesiastes 3:1-8), but when it is time to laugh, laugh a lot. Laughter is a medicine that we cannot overdose on and has no side effects. Enjoy the medicine of laughter today, maybe even give some to others.

There are different reasons for laughter, like over something funny or over something exciting. The laughter of excitement can be over an anniversary or a birthday or some other significant event. Such is the case when angels rejoice over someone coming to faith in Jesus (Luke 15:10). They laugh and rejoice with excitement. I like to say angels of God have a "conversion party" when someone gets saved in Christ (conversion, meaning converting from unbelief to belief). My wife and I had a conversion party for our twin boys upon them trusting in Jesus for salvation. We had cake, prayed, gave the Lord thanks, talked about what it means to be a Christian, then let them release balloons to the heavens as symbols of their lives now being in Christ in the heavenlies. And we laughed with great excitement!

# 17

# MORALITY MATTERS

*I*T WAS A ROUTINE assignment to check rest areas each shift, especially at night, as darkness seemed to encourage bad behavior at them. One night while rolling through a rest area, a local-plated pickup was noticed in the darkness of the exit. Suspicious over why a local vehicle would be there in the darkness, a closer look was warranted. Two adults having consensual sex were discovered. They were married, but not to each other. The woman remarked, "I feel terrible. We should not have done this. This will destroy our families." All sexual sin is destructive.

> *"Flee from sexual immorality. All other sins a man commits are outside his body, but he who sins sexually sins against his own body"*(1 Corinthians 6:18).

"Body" refers to the whole person, physically and spiritually. Though sin is sin, no other sin affects a person as sexual sin does. Satan knows the power and destruction of sexual sin, so he works hard to trap us in its web like a spider traps its prey. This devotional is not meant to address specific sexual sins, but to encourage each of us to take morality seriously. This includes all morality, not just sexual morality.

Flee sexual morality. Run from it. Literally or figuratively, put track shoes on your feet and run as hard and as far away from sexual sin as possible. My twin boys were good runners in school, winning multiple medals each. Win a medal, so to speak, for outrunning sexual sin. A practical way to combat sexual temptation is to change one's thought patterns. For example, instead of thinking about impure things, think about pure and right things (Philippians 4:8-9). Thankfully, all sin can be forgiven in Christ. Consequences remain, but the sin can be washed away by the cleansing power of Jesus.

Regarding morality in general, we live in a moral relativistic world in which morality is increasingly determined by society itself or individuals in society or societal culture. Absolutes are thrown out the window. To say there are no absolutes yet claim the absoluteness of moral relativism is a contradiction, however. This contradiction becomes apparent and moral relativism implodes when its adherents are subjected to their own beliefs and contradictions. For example, a government that believes its moral to commit genocide in a certain population of its people (moral relativism) would revolt against such actions if the government itself were the target (absolutes). A person who has no problem stealing from others (moral relativism) would insist on justice if others stole from him (absolutes). A person who champions "Defund the Police" and the ensuing crime wave in our nation (moral relativism) would dial 911 and rethink his stand on crime when the crime wave reached his front door (absolutes). Endless examples exist.

There are absolutes. All people know this, even moral relativists. God has written His moral code on our hearts (Romans 2:14-15). Like a sculpture etches stone, God etched His moral standards upon our souls. They are permanently imprinted on man's very being. In addition, Scripture reveals God's moral code (e.g., The Ten Commandments). What moral standard might you need to better uphold in your faith, life and world?

# 18

# CALL FOR BACKUP

LAW ENFORCEMENT OFFICERS CALL for backup, or assistance, whenever a situation warrants it, especially a situation involving a dangerous criminal. It's common for law enforcement officers to encounter threatening people and situations. An unwise practice of allowing someone in my front seat was about to change. While the man was seated in my car, dispatch responded to my initial check of his driver's license, saying, "10-35, 10-50 – advise." No Nebraska law enforcement officer wants to hear this. It is the worst report an officer can receive. The code means, "Subject wanted on an outstanding felony warrant, and is a most-dangerous offender." This means pucker-factor multiplied. So, trying to mask my startled emotions from the criminal seated next to me, I calmly asked him to return to his car to await a warning for speeding (I thought a warning vs. citation would divert any suspension of being arrested). Then I called for backup. Backup is a wise and needed officer safety practice.

Christians need backup too, though obviously not in the same way as law enforcement officers. Christians need one another. Scripture contains numerous "one another" passages that tell us the importance of being together, each one premised on the practice of regular gatherings, like church services. This is one reason the writer of the Book of Hebrews said this: *"Let us not give up meeting together, as some are in the habit of doing, but let us encourage one another — and all the more as you see the Day approaching"* (Hebrews 10:25). These words are in the immediate context of motivating one another toward greater love and good deeds because of what Christ has done for us. Again, this requires being together. Just as a family must be together to encourage one another, so Christians, the family of God, must gather to motivate and encourage each other.

More than simply being in church, be involved in the life of your church. Be more than just a warm body in pew, be an active participant. Surround yourself with God's people on a regular basis. Practice your faith in the context of church life. Give and receive encouragement. What happens when a hot briquet is taken from the fire? It cools down. Likewise, when a Christian is away from the life and fellowship of the church, he/she cools down. The flame of faith slowly dims.

Unless you have good reason to miss church, be there to give and receive many good things, like encouragement to keep your faith burning bright and hot.

Attending church is not all about you, but also about others – giving others encouragement and other good and needed things. We need each other. We need backup, especially as the end approaches. Satan knows this, and thus tries to keep us apart. He likes to keep us distant from one another at times when we need one another the most. Surely Satan loves COVID-19 because it has necessitated adapting church services accordingly, like meeting less or not meeting at all. We must figure out a way to obey God's command to meet while also honoring the government's requirements. Also, regarding COVID and Christians, it's realized there's strong disagreement over certain COVID related things, but we must come together in unity or continue to allow Satan to drive the wedge deeper. Maybe the answer is found in the biblical mandate of love. How should love for one another look in a COVID world? How should love for our neighbor look in a COVID world? Is Christian love part of the backup we need? Something to think about.

# 19

# EXCUSES

RIVERS OFTEN GAVE AN excuse for their heavy foot. Some excuses were quite ingenious, even almost believable – almost, like the case of the pregnant woman. I stopped a family traveling in two vans a few miles past a major freeway interchange for speeding. Upon existing my patrol car, the driver of one of the vans came running back to me, yelling, "My daughter is having a baby. She is about to go into labor. That's why we were driving fast." "Sounds fishy," I thought. Prudence demanded believing before dismissing. I rushed up to the van to find a woman who was indeed pregnant experiencing labored breathing. Still suspicious of the situation, I said, "How long has she been in labor?" The driver responded, "At least several minutes." Then I said, "You just pasted a major freeway interchange one mile back with a big sign reading, 'Hospital.' Your story is bogus. She's obviously pregnant, but she is not in labor. It's all a show to get out of a speeding ticket." The driver said, "Okay, you got us," and the pregnant woman quit breathing heavy and said, "Can't blame us for trying." Busted! They were without excuse.

Mankind gives God many excuses for not believing in Him, but Scripture tells us we are without excuse. *"The wrath of God is being revealed from heaven against all the godlessness and wickedness of men who suppress the truth by their wickedness, since what may be known about God is plain to them, because God has made it plain to them. For since the creation of the world God's invisible qualities - his eternal power and divine nature - have been clearly seen, being understood from what has been made, so that men are without excuse"* (Romans 1:18-20). This means creation reveals the Creator God so clearly that we are without excuse for not believing. An honest look up at the heavens and out at the earth provides us with a clear and visible picture of the existence of God. Take time to ponder the wonders of the universe, like its vastness, order and beauty. Stand in awe of the Creator as you look at the stars in the night sky. Appreciate God's handiwork. Do the same with the earth and the things on earth. There is nothing like earth in the whole universe (Genesis 1:1).

Personally, I like to look at the heavens at night through binoculars on occasion. It's amazing how many more stars can be seen through just binoculars. Binoculars also provide a great view of the moon. Whether a telescope, binoculars or the naked eye, look at the heavens and consider the following: *"The heavens declare the glory of God; the skies proclaim the work of his hands.*

> *Day after day they pour forth speech; night after night they display knowledge. There is no speech or language where their voice is not heard. Their voice goes out into all the earth, their words to the ends of the world"* (Psalm 19:1-4).

There is no excuse for not believing in the existence of God and, if God, His Son too, whom He sent to die for our sins and rise from the dead to save us. *Knowing God exists is not enough to be saved from sin and see heaven. We must trust in Jesus to get to heaven. I know the President of the United States exists, but to have a personal relationship with him I must go through his Chief of Staff. Likewise, to see God I must go through His Son, Jesus. Christ said, *"I am the way and the truth and the life. No one comes to the Father except through me"* (John 14:6). Do not suppress this truth.

# 20

# STAY IN THE BATTLE

*A* MAN ARRESTED FOR DRIVING
while intoxicated with alcohol
took the case to court. My testi-
mony on the witness stand took four hours. The
defendant also took the stand, confessing in a
court of law in front of a jury of his peers that
he was in fact driving on a public roadway while
over the legal limit of alcohol, yet the jury found
him "not guilty." The verdict left me dumb
founded, disillusioned and mad. Life was risked
in arresting the defendant, correct sobriety tests
were followed, all departmental and legal procedures were upheld, he admitted his guilt, yet was
released. Upon arriving home, I thought, "Why
fight a battle on the streets when something like
this happens?" I wanted to quit. A friend and fellow cop encouraged me to stay in the battle. I
did not exit law enforcement until God led me
into a different battle – the battle for souls.

The Christian life is a battle, one that sometimes
deflates us. We experience an attack against our

faith or come up against an agonizing situation or see no or little fruit from our efforts to minister to others, or someone wounds us, and we feel like quitting. This is when we need other Christians the most. We need their encouragement and support to stay in the fight.

*"Fight the good fight of the faith. Take hold of the eternal life to which you were called when you made your good confession in the presence of many witnesses"* (1 Timothy 6:12). Using athletic imagery, Paul, the penman, tells us here to fight like a boxer or wrestler or runner to some other athlete. Like any athletic competition, the Christian life is sometimes an agonizing and demanding fight, but a good one. So, literally, keep on fighting it. Stay in the battle.

Though the Christian life may exhaust or deflate you at times, stay in the battle. When Satan pins you to the mat, get back up and fight another day. When some experience zaps your strength and spirit, reenergize by the word of God and the people of God. When persecuted or attacked, remember what Jesus suffered for you. Christ stayed in the battle to bring us salvation. Let us stay in the battle to honor His sacrifice. This is not a battle to acquire or gain salvation, but a battle because of salvation. We do not fight to earn salvation but because we have salvation.

Part of this fight involves sharing our faith in Christ with others. Telling someone about Jesus can be quite hard at times, feeling like a battle of sorts, at least an inward one. But people must hear the Gospel to be saved by the Gospel (Romans 10:14-15). I share the following three principles to help and encourage you to share Jesus with others: 1) Relax. Your work is to share not save. Only God can save; 2) Remember. Your work is to be yourself not someone else. For example, tell your story of faith in Christ not someone else's; 3) Relate. Your work is to listen and connect not push and impose. As you relate and build a relationship with someone, you will have natural opportunity to share the Gospel. Stay in the battle for souls and soul-growth, including your own.

# 21

# TRUE IDENTITY

*A*REPORT WAS RECEIVED TO watch for two individuals wanted for recent murders in Denver, Colorado. They were driving a green-colored Ford Bronco with Colorado license plates thought to be headed east from Colorado into and through Nebraska. They were spotted within an hour of the report. Backup was called. The vehicle was stopped felony style – shotguns drawn and ready. After handcuffing the suspects and doing a thorough identity investigation, they were found not to be the true suspects. These innocent persons just happen to be driving a similar vehicle and had similar physical appearances. Their true identify did not match that of the actual suspects, so they were released with deepest apologies.

Identity in Christ is written in stone. There's no mistaking it. He is the Rock of our salvation (Psalm 18:2). This identity also has multiple characteristics, too many to list here, but summarized in Galatians 2:20. *"I have been cruci-fied with Christ and I no longer live, but Christ lives in me. The life I live in the body, I live by faith in the Son of God, who loved me and gave himself for me"* (Galatians 2:20). The truth that Jesus lives in believers encapsulates our identity in Him. Christ in us expresses the essential features of who we are in Him. We are not Christ, but iden-tified with Him, and thus have many blessings and promises as outlined in Scripture. It's kind of like saying you are not your father, but you are identified with him, and have many bless-ings and promises because of him.

But Satan wants you to be mis-identified. He wants you to doubt and question your identity in Christ. For example, Satan works to convince you that you are not forgiven, not redeemed, not righteous, not a child of God, not made new, not heir with Christ, not secure, not loved, not a beautiful creation, not headed to heaven, and so on. Go to Scripture and discover, or re-discov-er, your identity in Jesus. Believe these things, not the things Satan and/or the world tells you. Investigate the Bible to see how God identifies you in Christ. Dig into the word of God and be amazed at your uniqueness in Jesus. The deeper you dig into and investigate Scripture, the more you will see your true identity in the One who died and rose to forgive you and give you eternal life. His name is Jesus. He gave Himself for you.

We all remember getting separated from our mother somewhere as a child. It was frightening. But then we heard our mother's voice – her unique voice that clearly identified her, and we were relieved to be reunited. God's voice is contained in Scripture. If you ever feel distant from Him, listen to His voice calling from His word – His unique voice that clearly identifies both Him and you, and be relieved to be reunited. Of course, God never leaves us, we only think He has at times.

We're also familiar with what it means to be a "card carrying member" of something. Christians are card carrying members of heaven, so to speak. The card is made of the blood of Christ with God's signature on it alongside our name. The card is called The Lamb's book of life (Revelation 21:22-27). Those who believe in Jesus have their names in this book. Jesus is your true identity.

# 22

# LISTEN TO GOOD REASON

*A*N ILLINOIS PLATED VAN was clocked traveling eastbound at a high speed. A strong odor of marijuana poured out of the driver's window as he rolled it down to hand out his license and other pertinent documents. There were several passengers in the van as well. The group of executives of a Fortune 500 company in Chicago were returning from a snow skiing trip in Colorado. I asked, "Okay, where's the marijuana?" The driver responded, "What marijuana?" A few passengers then chimed in saying, "We don't even smoke the stuff." Response: "I want you to think hard about what I'm about to say. You have a choice to make. You can either hand over the marijuana or I can search for it. If I search for it, you will be arrested. Then you can call your company CEO and explain why his executives are in jail and the company van stored in a Nebraska State Patrol impound lot. Your choice. Think about it." They quickly handed over the marijuana. The group's proper response to reason spared them a lot of misery, possibly their jobs. Reason can be a powerful tool.

> *"Now while Paul was waiting for them [Silas and Timothy] at Athens, his spirit was provoked within him as he saw that the city was full of idols. So he reasoned in the synagogue with the Jews and the devout persons, and in the marketplace every day with those who were there"* (Acts 17:16-17).

The context goes on to tell us that Paul told the people their foreign gods and idols were worthless, and they needed to reach out to God, the Creator of all things. While being sensitive to the people's beliefs, Paul gave them the true gospel, providing enough information so they could make an informed decision. In other words, people of Athens, "I hear you, and here's what you need to know. . . Now think about it."

Give others enough information so they can make an informed decision. Reason with them. Of course, listen when others reason with you. Reason is a two-sided coin. We give and receive reason. Some people want to just speak. They are slow to listen and quick to talk, but a wise person gives and, especially, receives good reason.

Do you listen to good reason? Reason does not replace faith, but reason can bring us closer to faith in Christ.

Consider the following regarding heaven and hell. Heaven is real. Hell is real. We go to one place or the other upon death (Luke 16:19-31). Those who trust in Jesus go to heaven and others to the latter (John 3). Heaven is paradise. Hell is misery. And there is ample historical and biblical evidence to show that Jesus is real. Thus, good reason concludes the best choice is heaven through Jesus.

Some people do not think there is a hell, or at least do not want there to be one. But just as a moral society has punishment for those who act outside the law, so there is a hell for those who refuse God's provision of Christ as the only means to heaven. Other people might think, "Why would a loving God send anyone to hell?" When a child misbehaves who really grounds him/her – the parents or the child? Loving parents simply act on the child's choice/behavior. Likewise, a loving God acts on our choice, belief or unbelief in His Son, Jesus. In unbelief we effectively, if you will, ground ourselves in hell.

# THE BIG PICTURE

*E*VERY JOB HAS A big picture, a larger goal or purpose. The Nebraska State Patrol's big picture is contained in its motto, "Pro Bono Publico" - "For the Good of the Public." Keeping this larger picture of the job in mind was easy when things were good, but when things were bad, well, it was tested. I had to labor to remember the big picture of the job when, for example, patrolling in bad weather or dealing with difficult people or when being verbally and/or physically assaulted. I tried my best under such things to uphold public safety and perform my duties for the good of the public.

Several incidents tested the big picture, like a woman who threw all kinds of things at me for stopping her for speeding. She was clocked in a snowstorm at 90 MPH. "She is going to kill herself and/or others if she's not slowed down, especially in these adverse conditions," I thought. After stopping and informing her of her reckless driving, she threw a hairbrush at me while cussing. Other items from her car followed. She grabbed anything and everything to throw, including a pen, book, cup holder, makeup kit, and a myriad of things from her purse. As each item moved through the air at great speed out the window toward me, it was followed by a different curse word or phrase. She was mad. But I kept my cool, remembering the larger picture of public safety. Her insults were endured for the good of the public, including her own good. After the incident, I thought, "In the end, it all works together to keep people safe."

God has the biggest picture of all. For example, the Lord works everything together for the good of His people.

> *"And we know that in all things God works for the good of those who love him, who have been called according to his purpose. For those God foreknew he also predestined to be conformed to the likeness of his Son, that he might be the firstborn among many brothers. And those he predestined, he also called; those he called, he also justified; those he justified, he also glorified. What, then, shall we say in response to this? If God is for us,*

> *who can be against us?"* (Romans
> 8:28-31).

Notice, the text says, "all things." This means
even bad things, like illness or loss. Bad things
do not become good, however, but God promises to use them for our good. Just as failing a test
in school is not in itself good but can spur us to
study more and in this sense work for good, so
experiencing bad things are not in themselves
good but can ultimately work for our good. This
good is making us more like Jesus. God uses everything in our lives to make us more like Christ.
Therefore, all things work for us not against us.

Keep the big picture that God uses everything
in your life for your good in mind as you live
your life. Remember the larger goal of becoming more like Jesus when you experience bad
things. Doing so will help you accept the ugly
side of life, especially when ugly things happen
to you personally. What unpleasant thing might
you be experiencing today? Is there a trial at the
doorstep of your life? Trials are funny things –
we're either going into a trial or experiencing a
trial or coming out of a trial. A trial of some kind
is always on us or about to be on us. Whatever
the case, adopt the biblical perspective that all
things ultimately work for the good of making
God's children more like Jesus. Admittedly, no

trial is fun or enjoyable, but, thankfully, God has the big picture in mind and is always working to bring it about in our lives. Trust Him.

Think of a puzzle. God works to place each piece perfectly in our lives toward realizing the complete picture – the big picture that He already sees.

# 24

# PASS THE TORCH

*E*ACH NEBRASKA STATE PATROL training camp is an exercise in passing the torch of state law enforcement to recruits, the next generation of crime fighters. Passing the torch of law enforcement to others is a matter taken seriously by both trainers and recruits. The training involves all aspects of law enforcement, including emergency vehicle operation, weapons, defensive tactics, law, court testimony, first responder, sobriety testing, technology, arrest procedures, patrolling procedures, equipment care, radar, drug enforcement, accident investigation, and other things. I enjoyed all aspects of training. Those days are long in the past but still crisp in the mind's memory bank. I thank the state patrol for allowing me to carry the torch of law enforcement and hopefully passing it to others during time served.

We pass many things to others in life. The most important thing we can pass to another person is knowledge about Jesus and His word.

*"Hear, O Israel: The Lord our God, the Lord is one. Love the Lord your God with all your heart and with all your soul and with all your strength. These commandments that I give you today are to be upon your hearts. Impress them on your children. Talk about them when you sit at home and when you walk along the road, when you lie down and when you get up. Tie them as symbols on your hands and bind them on your foreheads. Write them on the doorframes of your houses and on your gates"* (Deuteronomy 6:4-9).

Though written specifically to Israel, this has application or profit to all the children of God.

Pass the torch of faith in Christ to others, beginning with your family. Live the word of God. Impress Jesus on the hearts of your children. Talk about Jesus and His word at home, making application to life in and out of the home. Jesus should be the centerpiece of your life and household. Raise your children to know and follow Jesus (Ephesians 6:4). Something is being passed to your children; the world passes unbelief to them, for example. Get to your children before others do. Instruct your children in what matters most – Jesus. Of all the things you might pass to your children and others, pass the torch of faith. Tell them about the saving desire and power of Christ. Model the Christian faith. Help others walk in Christ.

By the way, children can understand even deep spiritual things, so do not be afraid to talk about deep matters of faith with them. I remember, for example, my twin boys standing in our yard looking up to the heavens at the tender age of four, saying, "We are looking for Jesus to return in the clouds as the bible says He will." Children even comprehend more than adults at times spiritually because they do not have our spiritual baggage to offload before seeing clearly. My point to start instructing your children in the things of Jesus at an early age. Whatever the age of your children, start today. It's never too late to begin. Start passing the torch or fan the flame of the torch brighter today.

We've all seen the Olympic Torch Run, or Relay. It's impressive to see athletes hold the flame high as they run to pass it to successive runners as it moves closer the Olympic cauldron for the opening ceremony. The flame of faith in Christ should be held high. Keep the flame burning brightly. Pass the flame to others.

# 25

# IMPOSTORS

*D*RIVERS OCCASIONALLY PRE-
SENTED FAKE United States citi-
zenship papers with fake identifica-
tion cards, even fake driver's licenses. One such
case involved numerous people, over twenty.
No one had proper identification. A close look
at each person's identification revealed fraud in
each case. They were impostors, appearing to be
U. S. citizens when in fact they were not. Oh,
this happened at night with no back-up. Twenty-
some people against one. The One referred to
here was not me, but the Lord. My survival was
in His hands. I often wonder if these offenders
saw something or someone near me, like a host
of holy angels ready to do battle? There were
many situations in which the only explanation
for survival was the Lord God above. I'm grateful to the Lord for His protection, including
deliverance from multiple impostors on a dark
night.

Spiritually speaking, many imposters exist in the world. From false religions to false teachers to false teachings, imposters scatter the spiritual landscape of the globe with Satan behind each one. Satan tries to pass his fakes off as the real deal.

> *"For such men are false apostles, deceitful workmen, masquerading as apostles of Christ. And no wonder, for Satan himself masquerades as an angel of light. It is not surprising, then, if his servants masquerade as servants of righteousness"* (2 Corinthians 11:13-15).

Satan wears a mask to try to hide his darkness. This mask first appears as light but upon closer scrutiny is revealed to be dark. For example, Satan tells people they are too bad to be forgiven of their sins. The truth is that, yes, we are sinful people who have done bad things, but Jesus forgives all sin when we come to Him in faith (Colossians 2:13-15). Or consider Satan's lie that it is okay to boil with anger for an extended period. The truth is that anger itself is not sinful, but it must be appropriately managed in a timely way (Ephesians 4:26-27). Satan tells many lies, each one with a kernel of truth imbedded to make it first appear believable. Evaluate all things by the truth of God's word. Listen to God's voice as spoken in His revealed word, the Bible. Look closely at things. Inspect the fine print of spiritual claims.

Familiarize yourself with the word of God. Know what God's word says. Test all spiritual things against the Scriptures. Knowing what the Bible teaches will help you identify counterfeit teachings. Remember, Satan is always trying to deceive you in some way by presenting himself as light, so test it by the true light – the light of Christ and His word. Satan counterfeits everything Christian, so evaluate everything presented as Christian by the true light of the Scriptures.

If you were lost in the total darkness of a cave and two people showed up with flashlights, one a knock-off with no real, lasting light and the other a true light to show the path to safety, which would you follow? The person with the true light, of course. Satan is a knock-off. God is the true light. Follow Him. Or consider the age-old game we all played as children - hide-n-seek. My family's version gave the person at base a flashlight. The flashlight provided a great advantage for finding others hid in the darkness. Scripture is our advantage in spotting things hid in darkness, namely, Satan's lies. Use the truth and light

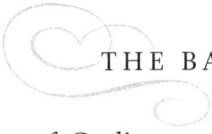

of God's word to expose darkness (Ephesians 5:11), including darkness in your own life.

# 26

# BAD DECISIONS

A LARGE WILD MARIJUANA PATCH existed in the area. The patch could be accessed only from two points, a north entrance and a south one. Occasionally, troopers were stationed at both ends while other troopers drove to the patch to flush out any harvesters of the illegal substance. During one of these operations, a young man was flushed from the patch my direction. There was no hope of escape. Upon contacting the young man, it was discovered he harvested enough of the wild and illegal crop of marijuana to fill a large duffle bag, probably, as I remember, thirty or forty pounds of the stuff. The young man was asked why he was doing this? He responded, "I learned of this patch on the streets of Denver, Colorado, and that a duffle bag of it would pay for my college education. Guess I made a poor choice." The lad's decision costs him greatly, beginning with jail instead of college. Law enforcement officers encounter people who made bad choices daily. Poor decision making is one reason we need law enforcement.

Scripture is saturated with examples of poor decision making. The Bible is painfully honest about the dumb things we choose to do at times. No matter who we are, all of us have made bad choices in our lives. I am not talking about mistakes, as in mistakenly driving the wrong way on a one-way street. Neither am I addressing poor choices, like watching a bad movie. Rather, I am addressing decisions that arise from the soil of sin in our lives. Sin is like bad dirt – it produces weeds. For example, the bad dirt of a depraved mind produces the weeds of fornication and adultery. Thankfully, we can learn from bad choices to move forward to make better ones.

After protecting an adulterous woman from a sure death by stoning from a pack of murderous and hypocritical men, Jesus said to her, *"Go now and leave your life of sin"* (John 8:11). Jesus defended not her behavior, but her as a person, and instructed her to quit committing adultery. The implication of the text is that she learned a hard lesson and left her sinful lifestyle upon being forgiven by Jesus. She learned from bad choices to move forward to make better ones motivated by the grace of the Savior.

Move forward from bad decisions. Do not get stuck in the mud of wrong moves. Leave sin behind and strive for righteousness. For example, learn to think before speaking upon saying something you regret. Learn to tell the truth when caught in a lie. Learn to be content with what you have after emptying your savings account for something you really did not need. Learn to make better use of the opportunities God gives you upon realizing wasted ones. Learn to forgive others after feeling the weight of unforgiveness. Learn to properly deal with anger after harboring it. Especially, learn to receive Christ's forgiveness for bad decisions and move forward in life and faith.

When addressing his own bad choices and failures, Paul said, *"I press on. Forgetting what is behind and straining toward what is ahead, I press on toward the goal to win the prize for which God has called me heavenward in Christ Jesus"* (Philippians 3:12-14). Paul doesn't mean forget as in never recall, but forget as in don't wallow in the past like a pig wallows in mud. If it helps, think of traveling down the road in a car – the rearview mirror is the past, the inside of the car the present, and the looking through the windshield is the future. Be aware of the past while living in the present with an eye on the future.

# 27

# TINTED WINDOWS

*A* MAN WAS THREATENING TRAVELERS with a steel pipe in daylight hours at a rest area. He was running wildly and brandishing the pipe as to cause others harm. The suspect spotted me and dashed for a parked van that had extremely dark tinted windows, which in daylight hours were impossible to see through. He lunged for the side door of the van that someone on the inside opened for him, and lunged inside. I now knew the van contained at least two occupants. Cautiously, with weapon drawn, I yanked the side door open to see not two people but four. Because of the threatening report and situation, I shouted, "I will shoot if you move." The occupants froze. Like these hoodlums who tried to hide themselves behind tinted windows, we sometimes hide ourselves in darkness. This is especially true of spiritual matters.

> *"This is the verdict: Light has come into the world, but men loved*

> *darkness instead of light because their deeds were evil. Everyone who does evil hates the light, and will not come into the light for fear that his deeds will be exposed. But whoever lives by the truth comes into the light, so that it may be seen plainly that what he has done has been done through God"* (John 3:19-21).

The Light here is Jesus and His word. Jesus is real, but some people will not trust in Him because they prefer darkness. They hate the light of the truth of God's word, shying away because it reveals their sin. They prefer to live behind tinted windows. Conversely, some people trust in Jesus and live by the light of His word. This light is seen in their lives, just as darkness is visible in the lives of those who live in it.

Consider the terminator line of the moon that separates light and darkness. In a similar way, all people exist on one side of the, if you will, spiritual terminator line – light or darkness. Where are you?

Don't hide behind the tinted windows of sin. Come out of the darkness into the light of Christ. Invite Jesus and His word to reveal your dark side. Let Christ and the Scriptures transform you into an ever-growing and glowing light. As this light grows and glows in your life, more and more darkness will be dispelled helping you see things anew and do things for the glory of God and the good of others like you never thought possible. You will grow as a Christian and in doing Christian things. Consider lightbulbs. They push away darkness. Jesus is the Light of the world; He pushes away darkness. Trust in Him. Follow Him. Immerse yourself in His word. Allow Jesus to, if you will, change the dead light bulbs of your soul – the tinted windows of your spirit to something that is bright, warm and alive.

Jesus spoke to a crowd that witnessed Him forgive and restore a repentant woman from the darkness of sin, saying, *"I am the light of the world. Whoever follows me will never walk in darkness, but will have the light of life"* (John 8:12). Christians will never be in complete darkness again. We don't need to live behind tinted windows. Rather, we have light and life, eternal light and life.

# 28

# UNLOVING ACT

*T*HE FOLLOWING ENCOUNTER WAS hard to believe. Something about a moving van towing a car appeared "off." The towed vehicle appeared to have a little girl in the driver's seat. "Maybe it's a doll," I thought. A closer look revealed a real girl. The van was immediately pulled over and the driver questioned after checking on the welfare of the girl. "Why is your child in this dangerous situation? This act is not only illegal and dangerous, but, in my mind, unloving." The father's behavior in the encounter was, well, weird, almost as if he cared more about getting down the road than he did about the well-being of his daughter, so a deeper investigation was pursued. The father was found to be wanted by the United States Military. Two military officers from the Pentagon were in Nebraska the next day to take custody of him. These military officers said it would be a long time, if ever, before his wife and daughter would see him again. This man's unloving act toward his daughter got him busted.

How often do we behave in an unloving way toward our family and/or others? I know my behavior is less than loving at times. God has a lot to say about love in Scripture: He is love; in love sent His Son to die for our sins; and we are expected to love Him and others, especially the family of God.

> *"Dear friends, let us love one another, for love comes from God. Everyone who loves has been born of God and knows God. Whoever does not love does not know God, because God is love. This is how God showed his love among us: He sent his one and only Son into the world that we might live through him. This is love: not that we loved God, but that he loved us and sent his Son as an atoning sacrifice for our sins. Dear friends, since God so loved us, we also ought to love one another. No one has ever seen God; but if we love one another, God lives in us and his love is made complete in us"* (1 John 4:7-12).

In a nutshell, God tells us here that a true Christian loves God, Jesus and other Christians. This does not mean we never act unloving, only that genuine love is part of who we are to the point that when behaving otherwise we will be quick to repent.

Love can be applied endless ways both in and out of the home and church, like praying for one another, serving one another, forgiving one another, worshipping with one another, reconciling with one another, greeting one another, encouraging one another, teaching one another, fellowshipping with one another, sacrifice for one another, and many other things. Basically, be willing and available to minister to the needs of others, even if it means being interrupted from your daily routines and schedule. Let us exchange unloving attitudes and actions with loving ones before God pulls us over on the road of life to make necessary corrections. We all have much to learn about loving as Jesus loves.

Far too often our words, attitudes and behaviors are attacking, harmful and unloving. For example, how do you view someone who does not believe as you believe? How do you treat an LGBT person? What if someone of a different color and culture walked into your church service? Do you see all people as being created in the image of God or just people of your likeness? Love is not put to the test with the familiar but with the unfamiliar. Did I show love toward the father in the above account? No. I could have and should have showed him the love of Christ while performing my duty to arrest him.

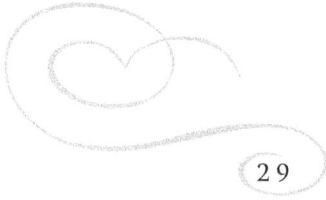

# 29

# THE WRONG WAY

CAR WAS TRAVELING WEST-
BOUND in eastbound lanes. I
sped to the area to find an older
woman driving her car the wrong way on the
interstate. Traffic was heavy and, thankfully,
taking evasive action to avoid an accident(s). I
pulled up alongside the woman's car to get her
attention to no avail. She would not divert her
eyes from the road to see me next to her as now
we both drove the wrong way. I had to get her
off the road for her safety and that of others,
so I gently contacted her car with my patrol car
and forced her off the road into the median. She
was safe. Others were safe. This elderly woman
still did not understand what happened, as she
said to me, "Hello young man. What are we doing here?" She was suffering from Alzheimer's.
As far as this woman was concerned, she was
doing a great job driving. She took the path that
seemed right to her, but it was a path that would
lead to destruction. Spiritually speaking, many

people take a road that seems right to them, but it is a road that leads to bad things.

*"There is a way that seems right to a man, but in the end it leads to death"* (Proverbs 14:12). Some people take the wrong path spiritually. They think upright and moral living, attending to religious duties, doing good to others, and giving to worthy causes is the right path, or road, to heaven. These things are good, but alone they do not get a person to heaven. There is but one way to heaven that is true, the way everlasting, the right and only road – Jesus. All other roads lead to eternal death, not to mention bad things along the way in this life.

Everyone is on a spiritual road of some type. What spiritual road are you travelling? Maybe your road is self-righteousness, trying to be good enough to get to heaven. Possibly, the spiritual road you are going down is religion itself. You might think being identified with a certain church and practicing spiritual rituals is the way to heaven. It may even be that your chosen road is good deeds, like doing enough good works will surely land you in heaven. Or it could be that you have elected unbelief in Christ as the way that seems right to you. Whatever the case, exit the road you are on and take the right one – Jesus. Jesus is not "a" way, as in one of many, but the only way. He is the one and only path to heaven. Even sincere belief in something false will not get you to heaven. The woman in the above account was sincere in her belief that she was going the right direction, but it would have led to her death in the end.

The Bible has a lot to say about Jesus being the only road to heaven, like in the Book of John. Read passages like John 3:16; 14:6; 11:25; and 20:31. Follow this up with Acts 4:12 and 1 Corinthians 15:3-4. Remember, this is God's word telling you empathically that Jesus is the one and only way to heaven. Do not take another road, no matter how good it may seem.

# 30

# DO NOT BE SURPRISED

*A* LARGE PART OF LAW enforcement training involves developing an attitude of not being surprised by things that happen while performing one's duty. Cops are taught to expect the unexpected, to prepare for worst-case scenarios. For example, a police officer is trained to anticipate and properly handle a person who suddenly resists arrest. Such was the case of a driver arrested for driving while intoxicated. He suddenly attached after field sobriety tests and impending arrest. The man did not catch me off-guard, though. He was taken down to the ground, cuffed, and transported to jail for processing. Thankfully, training taught me to anticipate such behaviors.

Christians, do not be surprised when the world attacks you. Do not be caught off-guard by hatred and opposition toward you. Trials of any kind should not startle us. In fact, we should anticipate them.

*"Do not be surprised, my broth-
ers, if the world hates you"* (1 John
3:13). *"Dear friends, do not be
surprised at the painful trial you
are suffering, as though something
strange were happening to you. But
rejoice that you participate in the
sufferings of Christ, so that you
may be overjoyed when his glory is
revealed"* (1 Peter 4:12-13).

Obviously, John and Peter are not talking about
trials brought about by our own making, like
when if we disobey the law, but trials that come
because we stand for Jesus, like being hated or
attacked for speaking truth. Do not be surprised
when these attacks happen. In fact, the godli-
er we live, the more we will be persecuted (2
Timothy 3:12).

The world is hostile to God and His people, so
do not be astounded when bad things happen to
God's people. Do not be dismayed when you experience suffering for living a Jesus-centered life
in an anti-Jesus world. For example, when you
choose to refrain from certain activities because
of your faith in Jesus, do not be shocked if others respond in a not-so-good way toward you.
How should Christians respond to this opposition? Love.

Reach out to the world in love for the cause of Christ. For example, as Jesus instructs us,

*"You have heard that it was said, 'Love your neighbor and hate your enemy.' But I tell you: Love your enemies and pray for those who persecute you"* (Matthew 5:43-44). Be good to those who cause you problems. As much as we should expect opposition to our faith in Jesus, we should also be ready to evidence proper attitudes and behaviors toward our attackers. This is hard to do at times, but, again, consider Jesus' example. We will never face hardship, trials and attacks like Christ did, therefore, we are without excuse for not showing His love toward others.

Love doesn't mean people shouldn't be held accountable for their actions, only that regardless of accountability or justice we are called to love. Love regardless. Love always. The biblical rule is to treat others as you want to be treated (Luke 6:31). Applying this precept to love, it means to love others as you want to be loved. Maybe we should love in such a way that it surprises others – love so radical that others take note (John 13:35).

# 31

# FORGIVENESS

*T*HIS DEVOTION APPEARS LAST because it has first importance. It emphasizes divine forgiveness. This is meant to leave you the reader with an indelible print of Christ's forgiveness. It does not matter who you are or what you have done, there is total forgiveness in Jesus Christ.

On certain occasions a driver was shown mercy upon the officer hearing what was believed to be a true confession, or admittance of guilt. One instance involved a driver who recently lost his wife to sudden death and was traveling to Colorado to be with children. I believed him, and in essence forgave him by issuing only a verbal warning. Likewise, God forgives us upon true confession.

> *"If we confess our sins, he is faithful and just and will forgive us our sins and purify us from all unrighteousness. If we claim we have not sinned, we make him out to be a*

*liar and his word has no place in our lives"* (1 John 1:9-10).

Though this was written to Christians, it has implication and application to anyone. We must confess our sins to be forgiven. Just as we had to acknowledge wrongdoing to our parents, we must admit our sin to God. To say we have not sinned is, well, lying. Lying to parents is one thing, lying to God another.

Do not lie to God. Rather, confess your sin and be forgiven. Again, it does not matter who you are or what you have done, there is total forgiveness in Christ. Jesus died on the Cross for our sins, was buried, then rose from the dead (1 Corinthians 15:3-4). For those who believe in Him, Jesus' death covers our sins (1 John 2:2) and His resurrection assures us eternal life (1 Corinthians 15:20-23). And this life everlasting can never be taken from you (John 10:27-30).

I close this devotional with one of the greatest promises in Scripture. Written to Christians, *"Praise be to the God and Father of our Lord Jesus Christ! In his great mercy he has given us new birth into a living hope through the resurrection of Jesus Christ from the dead, and into an inheritance that can never perish, spoil or fade - kept in heaven for you. who through faith are shielded by God's power until the coming of the salvation that is ready to be revealed in the last time"* (1 Peter 1:3-4). If you are a Christian, praise God the Father for Jesus the Son each day. Remember the Lord's great mercy toward you, including the truth that you possess the new birth (also see John 3:1-16) and resurrection that will not and cannot rot or go away because you are kept by God Himself!

If you are not a Christian, I hope you trust in Christ today. Confess to God that you are a sinner and that you believe Jesus died for your sins and rose from the dead. Then get connected with a Jesus-centered church. Read the Scriptures. Pray. Serve. Grow in Christ. Welcome to the family of God. See you in heaven, if not before! Oh, and have fun in life. Enjoy life. Christians have the most to celebrate and enjoy in life and eternity.

I leave you with the Mosaic priestly blessing: *"The Lord bless you and keep you; the Lord make his face shine upon you and be gracious to you; the Lord turn his face toward you and give you peace"* (Numbers 6:24-26).

www.ingramcontent.com/pod-product-compliance
Lightning Source LLC
Chambersburg PA
CBHW032006040426
42448CB00006B/496